The Ultimate Self-Teaching Method!

Play Piano Today! Worship Songbook

BOOK

Featuring 10 Contemporary Favorites!

ISBN 978-1-4584-0714-6

HAL•LEONARD®
CORPORATION

7777 W. BLUEMOUND RD. P.O. BOX 13819 MILWAUKEE, WI 53213

Visit Hal Leonard Online at
www.halleonard.com

Introduction

Welcome to the *Play Piano Today! Worship Songbook*. This book includes well-known worship favorites, and is intended for the beginner to intermediate player.

The ten songs in this book are carefully coordinated with the skills introduced in Level 1 of the *Play Piano Today!* method. Refer to the table of contents below to see where each song fits within the method and to help you determine when you're ready to play it.

Contents

About the CD

A full-band recording of every song in this book is included on the CD, so you can hear how it sounds and play along when you're ready. Each song is preceded by two measures of "clicks" to indicate the tempo and meter.

The CD is playable on any CD player, and is also enhanced so Mac and PC users can adjust the recording to any tempo without changing the pitch! For the latest Amazing Slow Downer software and installation instructions, go to **www.halleonard.com/ASD**.

Here I Am to Worship

Words and Music by Tim Hughes

The 𝄐 symbol is called a **fermata**. It means to hold the note(s) longer than the normal value.

Bind Us Together

Words and Music by Bob Gillman

Track 2

You Are My King
(Amazing Love)
Words and Music by Billy James Foote

Verse
Moderately fast ♩ = 132

I'm for-giv-en be-cause You were for-sak-en. I'm ac-cept-ed; You were con-

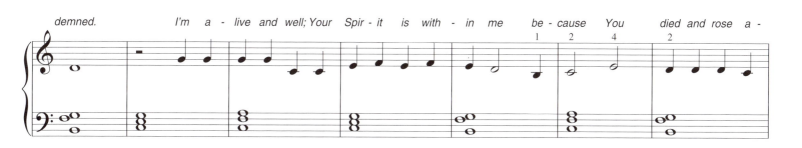

demned. I'm a-live and well; Your Spir-it is with-in me be-cause You died and rose a-

Chorus

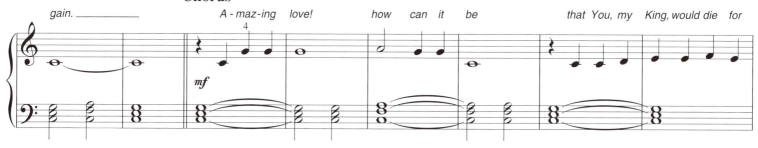

gain. A-maz-ing love! how can it be that You, my King, would die for

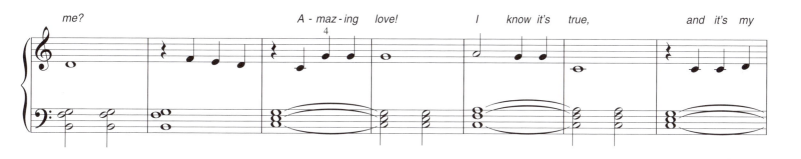

me? A-maz-ing love! I know it's true, and it's my

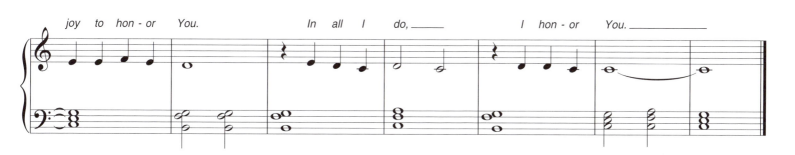

joy to hon-or You. In all I do, I hon-or You.

I Could Sing of Your Love Forever

Words and Music by Martin Smith

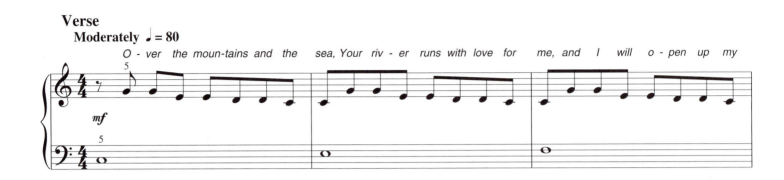

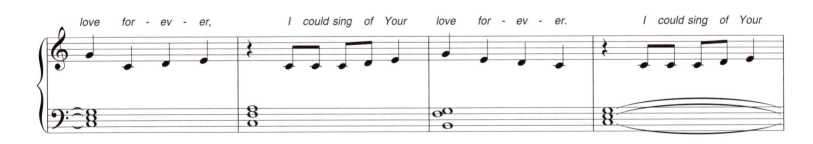

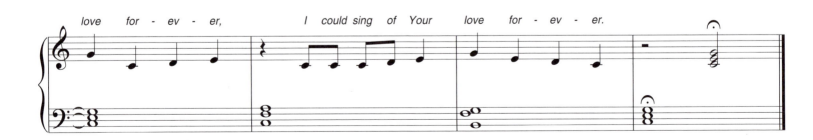

There Is a Redeemer

Words and Music by Melody Green

Verse

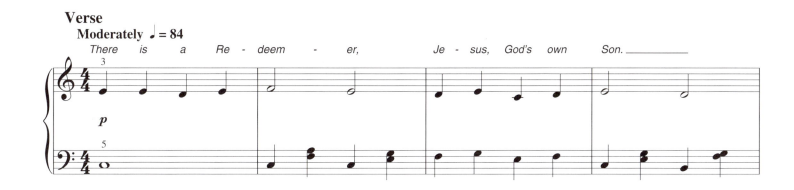

Chorus

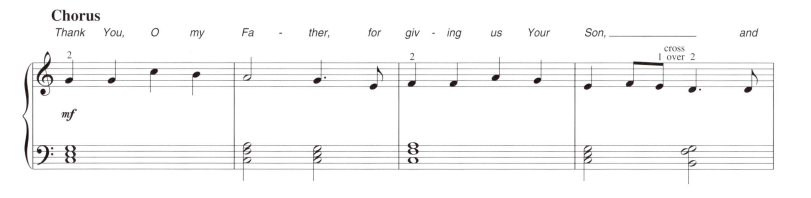

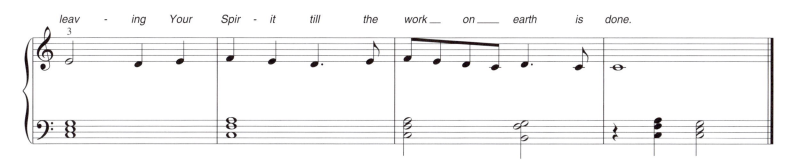

We Bow Down

Words and Music by Twila Paris

Track 6

Verse

With a lilt ♩ = 144

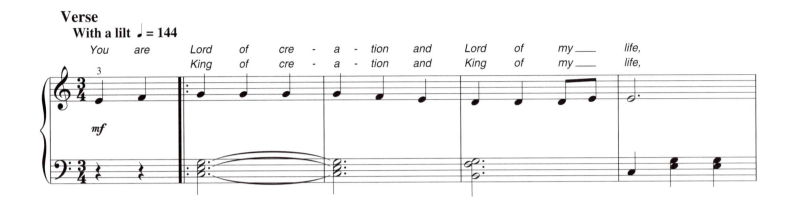

You are Lord of cre-a-tion and Lord of my ___ life,
King of cre-a-tion and King of my ___ life,

Lord of the land and the sea. You were
King of the land and the sea. You were

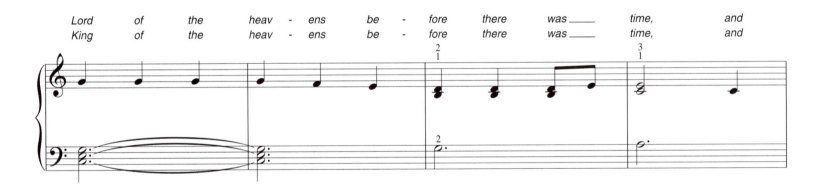

Lord of the heav-ens be-fore there was ___ time, and
King of the heav-ens be-fore there was ___ time, and

Lord of all lords You will be! We bow
King of all kings You will be! We bow

cross under

shift down

Chorus

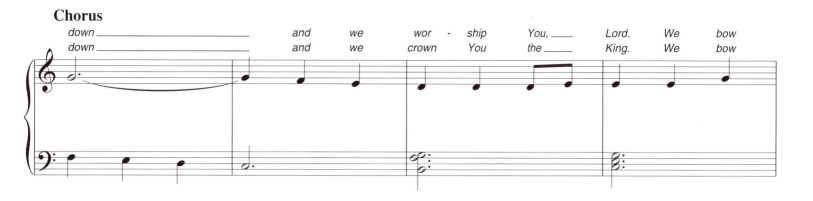

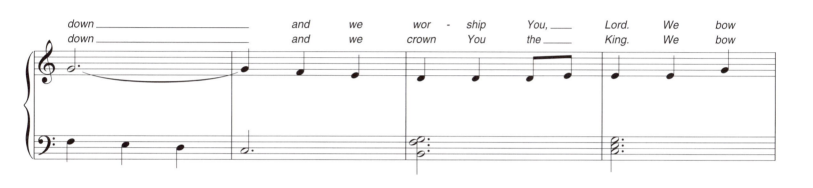

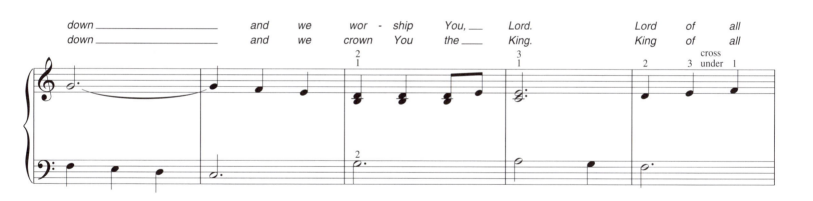

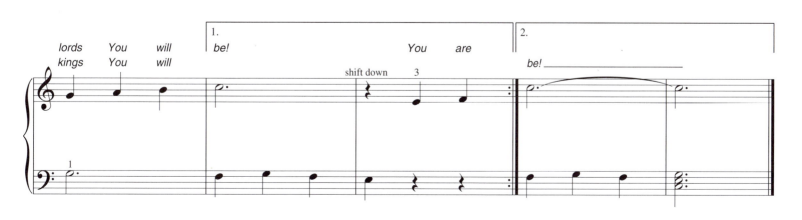

Spirit of the Living God

Words and Music by Daniel Iverson and Lowell Alexander

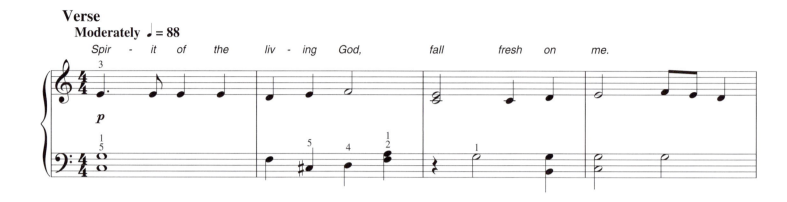

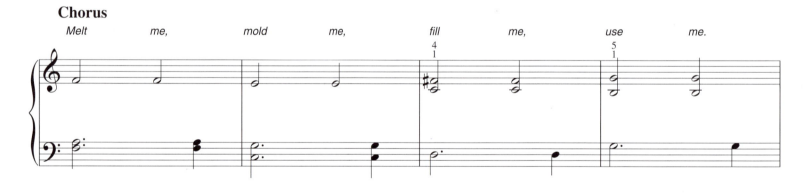

We Fall Down
Words and Music by Chris Tomlin

Awesome Is the Lord Most High

Words and Music by Chris Tomlin, Jesse Reeves, Cary Pierce and Jon Abel

(This page is left intentionally blank to eliminate a page turn.)

He Is Exalted

Words and Music by Twila Paris

Track 10

Chorus

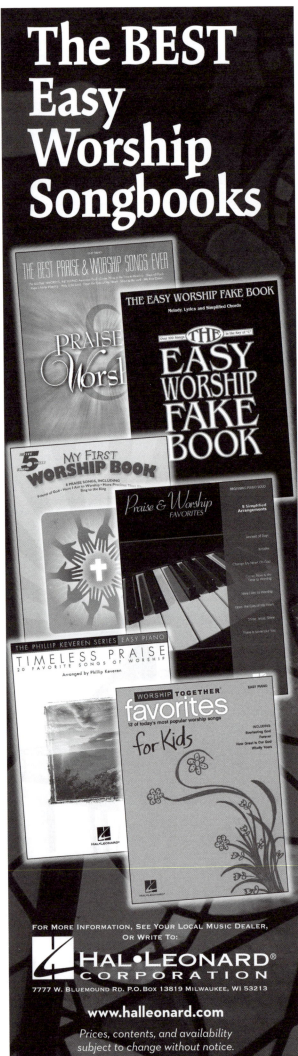

The BEST Easy Worship Songbooks

FOR MORE INFORMATION, SEE YOUR LOCAL MUSIC DEALER, OR WRITE TO:

HAL·LEONARD® CORPORATION
7777 W. BLUEMOUND RD. P.O. BOX 13819 MILWAUKEE, WI 53213

www.halleonard.com

Prices, contents, and availability subject to change without notice.

THE BEST PRAISE & WORSHIP SONGS EVER

74 all-time favorites: Awesome God • Breathe • Days of Elijah • Here I Am to Worship • I Could Sing of Your Love Forever • Open the Eyes of My Heart • Shout to the Lord • We Bow Down • dozens more.

00311312 P/V/G......................................$19.95

THE BIG-NOTE WORSHIP BOOK

20 worship tunes for beginning players, including: Agnus Dei • Days of Elijah • Everlasting God • Friend of God • Give Us Clean Hands • Here I Am to Worship • Mighty to Save • Open the Eyes of My Heart • Sing to the King • and more.

00311875 Big-Note Piano.........................$10.99

CONTEMPORARY WORSHIP FAVORITES

The Phillip Keveren Series
Easy arrangements of 15 powerful Christian favorites: Beautiful One • Better Is One Day • Breathe • Friend of God • Grace Flows Down • I Give You My Heart • Indescribable • Once Again • Revelation Song • The Wonderful Cross • and more.

00311805 Easy Piano...............................$12.95

THE EASY WORSHIP FAKE BOOK

This beginning fake book includes over 100 songs, all in the key of "C" with simplified chords. Songs include: Above All • Come, Now Is the Time to Worship • He Is Exalted • Lord, I Lift Your Name on High • You're Worthy of My Praise • and dozens more.

00240265 Melody/Lyrics/Chords $19.95

HERE I AM TO WORSHIP – FOR KIDS

This addition to the WorshipTogether series lets the kids join in on the best modern worship songs. Includes 20 favorites: Awesome God • Breathe • God of Wonders • He Is Exalted • Wonderful Maker • You Are My King (Amazing Love) • and more.

00316098 Easy Piano...............................$14.95

HOW GREAT IS OUR GOD

The Phillip Keveren Series
Keveren's big-note arrangements of 15 praise & worship favorites: Above All • Awesome God • Days of Elijah • Forever • Give Thanks • Here I Am to Worship • The Potter's Hand • Shout to the Lord • We Fall Down • more.

00311402 Big-Note Piano.........................$12.95

MODERN HYMNS

Easy piano arrangements of 20 contemporary worship favorites: Amazing Grace (My Chains Are Gone) • Before the Throne of God Above • How Deep the Father's Love for Us • In Christ Alone • Take My Life • The Wonderful Cross • and more.

00311859 Easy Piano...............................$12.99

MORE OF THE BEST PRAISE & WORSHIP SONGS EVER

Simplified arrangements of 80 more contemporary worship favorites, including: Beautiful One • Everlasting God • Friend of God • Hear Our Praises • In Christ Alone • The Power of Your Love • Your Grace Is Enough • Your Name • and more.

00311801 Easy Piano...............................$19.99

MY FIRST WORSHIP BOOK

Beginning pianists will love the five-finger piano format used in this songbook featuring eight worship favorites: Friend of God • Give Thanks • Here I Am to Worship • I Will Call Upon the Lord • More Precious Than Silver • Sing to the King • We Fall Down • and more.

00311874 Five-Finger Piano $7.99

PRAISE & WORSHIP FAVORITES

8 arrangements that even beginners can enjoy, including: Ancient of Days • Breathe • Change My Heart Oh God • Come, Now Is the Time to Worship • Here I Am to Worship • Open the Eyes of My Heart • Shine, Jesus, Shine • There Is None like You.

00311271 Beginning Piano Solo $9.95

TIMELESS PRAISE

The Phillip Keveren Series
20 songs of worship wonderfully arranged for easy piano by Phillip Keveren: As the Deer • El Shaddai • Give Thanks • How Beautiful • How Majestic Is Your Name • Lord, I Lift Your Name on High • Shine, Jesus, Shine • There Is a Redeemer • Thy Word • and more.

00310712 Easy Piano...............................$12.95

TODAY'S WORSHIP HITS

16 modern worship favorites, including: Amazed • Beautiful One • Days of Elijah • How Great Is Our God • Sing to the King • and more.

00311439 Easy Piano...............................$10.95

WORSHIP FAVORITES

20 powerful songs arranged for big-note piano: Above All • Forever • Here I Am to Worship • Open the Eyes of My Heart • Shout to the Lord • and dozens more.

00311207 Big-Note Piano.........................$10.95

WORSHIP TOGETHER FAVORITES FOR KIDS

This folio features 12 easy arrangements of today's most popular worship songs: Enough • Everlasting God • Forever • How Great Is Our God • Made to Worship • Mountain of God • Wholly Yours • The Wonderful Cross • Yes You Have • You Never Let Go • and more.

00316109 Easy Piano...............................$12.95

0809